The AI Gold Rush

HOW TO MAKE YOUR FIRST
MILLION WITH CHATGPT

BERNARD BADO

CONTENTS

Introduction

In just five days after its launch, ChatGPT hit a mind-blowing milestone of 1 million users. That's faster than Instagram, Twitter, or Facebook ever dreamed of growing. But here's the kicker: while everyone else is busy playing around with this shiny new toy, YOU have the chance to turn it into your own personal money-printing machine.

Listen, I've been in the tech game for years, and I'm telling you right now: ChatGPT isn't just another fad. It's a fucking revolution. It's like having a genius-level assistant, available 24/7, that never gets tired, never complains, and never asks for a raise. And the best part? It's yours to command.

Sam Altman, the big brain behind OpenAI, dropped a bomb that should make your entrepreneurial senses tingle: "There will be a one-man billion-dollar company." Let that sink in for a second. We're talking about the potential for a SINGLE person to build an empire worth billions. And guess what? That person could be YOU.

That's why I wrote this book. I'm here to show you how to leverage ChatGPT's insane capabilities to create not just one, but multiple income streams online. We're talking about practical, no-bullshit strategies that you can start implementing TODAY.

Now, you might be thinking, "Okay, but what can this AI really do?" It's like a Swiss Army knife for your business. It can write killer copy that converts like crazy, pump out SEO-optimized content faster than you can say "Google," and even code entire websites from scratch. It's like having a whole team of experts at your fingertips, ready to hustle 24/7.

And here's the beauty of it: You don't need to be some tech wizard or have an MBA to make this work. This book is for anyone with the guts to try something new and the drive to succeed. Whether you're:

- A stay-at-home parent looking to build a side hustle.

- A college student dreaming of launching the next big startup.

- Or a seasoned entrepreneur ready to 10x your existing business.

...this book has the blueprint you need to turn ChatGPT into your secret weapon for success.

Look, the AI revolution is here, and it's not slowing down. You can either watch from the sidelines as others cash in, or you can jump in and ride this wave to financial freedom. The choice is yours.

Remember: In the gold rush, it wasn't the miners who got rich—it was the people selling the shovels. ChatGPT is your shovel. Now let's go dig up some treasure.

My Free Gift to You

I'm about to drop some serious bonus content on you. Why? Because I love overdelivering, and I want you to win BIG.

So here's what you're getting, absolutely FREE:

My AI Newsletter: Every damn Sunday, I'm sliding into your inbox with the hottest ChatGPT and AI insights I've uncovered during the week.

My ChatGPT Prompts: I've built HUNDREDS of prompts that'll make ChatGPT sing, dance, and print money for you. Whether you're looking to create killer content, solve complex problems, or automate your business, these prompts are your secret weapon. And I'm handing them over to you on a silver platter.

Now, you might be thinking, "What's the catch?" There isn't one. I'm giving you the keys to the kingdom because I know that your success is my success. When you win, I win. It's that simple.

So, are you ready to level up? Grab your phone, scan that QR code on the next page, and get your bonuses.

Get Your Free Bonus!

Getting Started With ChatGPT

Now, let's talk about ChatGPT and how it can make you money.

Content Creation: ChatGPT can crank out blog posts, social media updates, and product descriptions that'll make your competitors weep. Imagine pumping out a month's worth of content in a single afternoon. That's the kind of productivity boost we're talking about here, folks.

24/7 Customer Service: Picture this - while you're sipping margaritas, ChatGPT is handling customer inquiries. It's like having a tireless support team that never needs coffee breaks or vacation days.

Market Research: Forget spending weeks poring over data. ChatGPT can analyze market trends faster than you can say "competitive advantage."

Idea Brainstorming: It can help you brainstorm new product ideas or marketing campaigns that'll have you smacking your forehead wondering, "Why didn't I think of that?" It's like having a whole think tank in your pocket.

Personalization: In today's market, one-size-fits-all is dead. ChatGPT can help you tailor your messaging to each customer like a bespoke suit. We're talking about the kind of personalization that turns casual browsers into loyal brand supporters.

Efficiency: Let's face it, there's never enough hours in the day. But with ChatGPT streamlining your emails, summarizing meetings, and helping with project planning, you'll suddenly find yourself with time to spare. And trust me, it feels like discovering a 25th hour in the day.

Here's the deal: whether you're a scrappy startup founder burning the midnight oil or a seasoned CEO looking to stay ahead of the curve, ChatGPT is your new secret weapon. It's not just about working harder; it's about working smarter. And trust me, this AI assistant is smarter than your average bear.

Think about it. How much more could you accomplish if you had a tireless assistant handling the grunt work while you focus on the big picture? That's the power of ChatGPT. It's not replacing you; it's supercharging you.

Now, I know what you're thinking. "Sounds great, but how do I actually use this to make money?" Well, buckle up, because in the next sections, we're diving deep into the nitty-gritty of using ChatGPT to make your first buck online.

But first, you need to learn how it works and how to use it.

Step 1: Create an account

First things first, let's get you armed and ready. Here's your battle plan:

1. Fire up your browser and head to chatgpt.com.
2. Look for the "Sign Up" button.
3. Follow the instructions to create your account.
4. Once you're in, take a moment to explore the interface. It's clean, it's simple, and it's about to become your best friend.

Step 2: Learning the Ropes

Alright, you're in the big leagues now. Time to learn how to swing that AI bat:

1. Look at the bottom of the screen. See that text box? That's where the magic happens.
2. Start simple. Type in a question like "What are 5 trending business ideas for 2024?"
3. Notice how quickly it responds? That's your new superpower. Use it wisely.
4. Now, let's kick it up a notch. Try this: "Write a 100-word product description for a smart water bottle that tracks hydration." Boom! Instant copywriting.

The key here is experimentation: Throw curveballs, fastballs, knuckleballs - see how ChatGPT handles them all.

Step 3: ChatGPT in Action

Let's put this bad boy into practice:

1. Imagine you're launching a new e-commerce store. Type in: "Create a 30-day content calendar for Instagram to promote a new athleisure brand."
2. Bam! You've got a month's worth of social media content planned in seconds. But don't stop there.
3. Follow up with: "Generate 5 catchy hashtags for each post in the content calendar."
4. You've just saved yourself hours of brainstorming and planning.

But here's where the real magic happens. Start combining prompts:

"Write a 500-word blog post about the benefits of sustainably made athleisure wear. Then, create 3 social media posts promoting this blog post, each optimized for Twitter, Facebook, and LinkedIn."

See what I did there? I'm not just using ChatGPT for one task - I'm chaining prompts together to create a whole marketing strategy. This is how you 10x your productivity, folks.

Now, here's your homework. Try these prompts on for size:

- "Develop a 5-step sales funnel for an online course about day trading."
- "Write 10 email subject lines that will skyrocket open rates for a new SaaS product."
- "Create a script for a 60-second TikTok video explaining NFTs to complete beginners."

Remember: ChatGPT is like a muscle - the more you use it, the stronger it gets. Or in this case, the smarter you get at using it.

How To Use ChatGPT

Effectively

Alright, hustlers. You've seen how ChatGPT works. Now we're gonna dive deep into the art of ChatGPT prompting.

Tip 1: Get Specific or Go Home

This is where 90% of the population mess up. They throw vague questions at ChatGPT like "How do I make money online?" and wonder why they're still broke. That's like walking into a Michelin-star restaurant and ordering "food." You gotta be specific as heck.

Instead of asking, "How do I promote my e-commerce store?", try this: "Create a 90-day marketing plan for launching a premium yoga mat brand, including weekly email newsletters, Instagram content strategy, influencer outreach targets, and KPIs for each channel."

See the difference? You're not just asking for ideas - you're demanding a whole darn blueprint.

Tip 2: Use The Frankenstein Strategy

This is where it gets fun. Start mashing up ideas like you're Dr. Frankenstein on a caffeine bender. The weirder the combo, the more potential for a unique response.

Try this on for size: "Write a blog post introduction that sounds like Deadpool wrote it. Use witty, romantic tone and pop culture references."

Crazy? Maybe. But that's exactly what creates unique outputs.

Tip 3: Refine, Reload, Repeat

If ChatGPT's first answer doesn't make you want to run to your laptop and start building an empire, don't settle. Push back. Demand more. It's like training a puppy - you gotta show it exactly what you want.

Example: "That blog post for my product is too vanilla. Make it more punchy and engaging for the readers"

ChatGPT gives you a new response.

You: "Now add three case studies of similar products and showcase how ours is better."

Keep pushing, keep going until you strike gold.

Tip 4: Shotgun Blast Your Way to Success

Here's a secret: don't just ask once. Ask the same question multiple times and watch the magic happen.

Try this: "Give me 10 unique e-commerce product ideas that combine tech gadgets with personal wellness, each targeting a different demographic."

Run it three times. Now you've got 30 potential million-dollar ideas. One of them could be your ticket to early retirement on a private island.

Remember: in this game, the spoils go to those who can out-think, out-hustle, and out-prompt everyone else.

Use ChatGPT To Become More Productive

Whether you're a solopreneur burning the midnight oil, a freelancer juggling clients like a circus act, or a startup founder wondering if sleep is just a myth - I'm talking to YOU.

You know the drill: too many hats to wear, not enough hours in the day, and a to-do list that breeds like rabbits. Sound familiar?

You're out there trying to conquer the world, but you're drowning in busywork. Writing emails, crafting social media posts, researching market trends, brainstorming product ideas - it's enough to make your head spin. And let's not even talk about the creative blocks. It's a wonder you haven't thrown your laptop out the window yet.

This is where ChatGPT makes your life a whole lot easier. It can handle everything from cranking out killer marketing copy to debugging your code, from brainstorming your next big idea to analyzing market trends.

And it's not just about saving time (though it'll do that in spades). It's about supercharging your productivity to levels you never thought possible.

Now, I know what you're thinking. "Sounds great, but how does this actually work in real life?" Glad you asked. In this chapter, I'm gonna show you exactly how.

We're talking real prompts, real responses, and real results. You'll see firsthand how tweaking your approach can mean the difference between a mediocre output and a golden nugget that could make you rich.

Disclaimer: I'll be showing full ChatGPT responses to show how much the result can change depending on your prompt. I'll also be cutting down long ChatGPT responses and only leave the important parts in.

Example 1: Write Emails

How many hours have you wasted trying to craft the perfect email that doesn't sound like it came from your grandma? And let's be real - how many times have you Googled "email templates" only to find cookie-cutter crap that wouldn't impress a wall, let alone a potential client?

Here's what separates the amateurs from the pros when it comes to writing emails:

1. **Personalization:** Generic emails are about as exciting as watching paint dry. You need to make that recipient feel like you're speaking directly to their soul.

2. **Hook:** Hit them with something juicy in the first sentence. Make them sit up and think, "Holy crap, I need to read this."
3. **Clear call-to-action:** Don't leave them hanging. Tell them exactly what you want them to do next, and make it so irresistible they can't help but click.
4. **A tone that resonates:** Whether you're going for professional cool or friendly fire, nail that tone like your business depends on it (because guess what, it does).

Now, imagine if you could nail all these elements every single time, without breaking a sweat or sacrificing your firstborn to the email gods. Enter ChatGPT, your new email-writing superpower.

Example: You're a fintech startup trying to reach out to the CEO of a major bank

Prompt: Write a cold outreach email for my fintech startup to the CEO of a major bank.

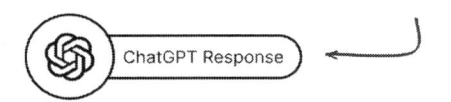

Subject: Unlock New Opportunities with [Your Fintech Startup Name]

Dear [CEO's Name],

I hope this message finds you well. I'm [Your Name], founder of [Your Fintech Startup Name]. Our cutting-edge platform is designed to streamline [specific service or benefit, e.g., digital payments, risk management, etc.], offering a seamless experience for banks like [Bank Name] to enhance customer engagement and operational efficiency.

I'd love to discuss how we can help [Bank Name] stay ahead in the rapidly evolving financial landscape. Could we schedule a brief call at your convenience?

Thank you for your time.

Best regards,
[Your Full Name]

[Your Contact Information]
[Your LinkedIn Profile or Website]

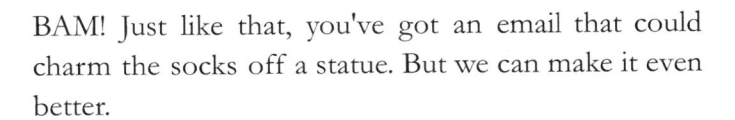

BAM! Just like that, you've got an email that could charm the socks off a statue. But we can make it even better.

Example: Make the email more engaging and personal.

Prompt: Make it more punchy and personalized.

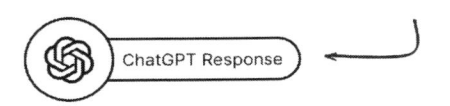

Subject: Transforming [Bank Name]'s Digital Future Together

Dear [CEO's Name],

I'm [Your Name], founder of [Your Fintech Startup Name], and I believe we can supercharge [Bank Name]'s digital strategy. Our platform is revolutionizing [specific service, e.g., digital payments, risk management], offering banks like yours a unique edge in customer engagement and efficiency.

Imagine [Bank Name] leading the charge in fintech innovation—let's make that happen. I'd love to share how we can drive this transformation together. Could we set up a quick call to explore the possibilities?

Looking forward to your thoughts.

Best,
[Your Full Name]
[Your Contact Information]
[Your LinkedIn Profile or Website]

This bad boy is more personal than your high school diary. It's not just "Dear Sir/Madam" garbage - it's speaking directly to the recipient. That's how you make someone sit up and take notice.

But we're about to kick it up another notch. You can tweak this bad boy even more. Want it funnier? Done. Need it more formal? Hell, you can even make it sound like J.K. Rowling wrote it.

Example: Write an email in the style of J.K. Rowling.

Prompt: Rewrite the email in the style of J.K. Rowling including Harry Potter references.

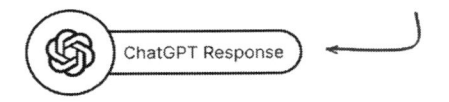 ChatGPT Response

Subject: A Magical Opportunity for [Bank Name]

Dear [CEO's Name],

I'm [Your Name], founder of [Your Fintech Startup Name], and I believe we're holding the wand that could cast a spell of innovation on [Bank Name]. Our platform is like the Marauder's Map for digital banking—revealing untapped opportunities and streamlining [specific service, e.g., digital payments, risk management] with the precision of a well-cast Expelliarmus.

Imagine [Bank Name] leading the Wizarding World of finance, with us as your trusted companions on this enchanted journey. Shall we conjure a brief meeting to discuss how we can work our magic together?

Awaiting your owl.

Best regards,
[Your Full Name]
[Your Contact Information]
[Your LinkedIn Profile or Website]

Example 2: Personal Training & Nutrition

Millions of people struggle to create the perfect balance of diet and exercise that'll transform their bodies from "meh" to "DAMN!" It's like trying to hit a curveball with your eyes closed - frustrating as hell and usually ending in disappointment.

You could spend hours combing through conflicting diet advice online, or spend big bucks for a personal trainer who'll yell at you for an hour a week. But who's got the time or money for that?

Example: Create a tailored diet plan.

Prompt: Act as a dietician. Your task is to give me a 4-week diet plan with caloric breakdown. I'm a male on a vegan diet. I'm 26 years old weighing 240 pounds and I'm 6 feet tall. My goal is to lose weight.

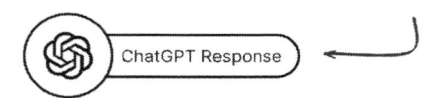

Caloric Breakdown:

- Calories per day: 2,000-2,200
- Protein: 20-25% (~100-130g)
- Carbohydrates: 45-50% (~225-275g)
- Fats: 25-30% (~55-75g)

Week 1 - Day 1

- Breakfast: Smoothie with 1 cup spinach, 1 banana, 1/2 cup blueberries, 1 tbsp chia seeds, and 1 cup almond milk (~300 calories)
- Snack: 1 apple with 2 tbsp almond butter (~250 calories)
- Lunch: Quinoa salad with 1 cup cooked quinoa, 1/2 cup chickpeas, cucumber, cherry tomatoes, and 1 tbsp olive oil (~500 calories)
- Snack: 1/4 cup mixed nuts (~200 calories)

- Dinner: Stir-fry with 1 cup tofu, mixed vegetables, 1 cup brown rice, and soy sauce (~600 calories)

Total: ~1,850 calories

Now that you've got your diet, let's get you moving. ChatGPT's got your back here too.

Example: Create a tailored workout plan.

Prompt: Keeping my diet and training goals in mind, generate a 3-day-a-week home workout plan.

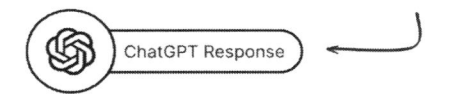

Day 1: Full-Body Strength + Cardio

Warm-Up (5-10 minutes):

- Jumping jacks
- Arm circles
- Leg swings
- High knees

Workout:

- Squats (Bodyweight or with resistance bands/dumbbells) - 3 sets of 12-15 reps
- Push-Ups (Modified if needed) - 3 sets of 10-12 reps
- Bent-Over Rows (With resistance bands or dumbbells) - 3 sets of 12-15 reps
- Lunges (Alternating legs) - 3 sets of 12-15 reps per leg
- Plank - 3 sets of 30-60 seconds
- Mountain Climbers - 3 sets of 30 seconds

Cardio Finisher (Optional):

- 30 seconds of burpees
- 30 seconds of rest

Cool-Down (5-10 minutes):

- Stretching all major muscle groups
- Focus on deep breathing

Just like that, you've got a workout routine that fits you like a glove. And here's the good part: ChatGPT remembers your meal plan, so it'll create workouts that fit well with your nutrition goals.

Example 3: Write Blog Posts

Creating high-quality content that doesn't put your readers to sleep is harder than convincing a cat to take a bath. It's a grind that can leave you feeling like you've gone 12 rounds with Mike Tyson... in his prime.

Traditionally, crafting a blog post that doesn't suck involves:

1. Brainstorming ideas
2. Researching your topic
3. Outlining your post
4. Writing the damn thing
5. Editing and proofreading

I know, it doesn't sound like fun at all. So let's see how ChatGPT can help here.

Example: Generate blog post ideas.

Prompt: Act as a keyword research tool. Find me 5 blog post ideas for relatively high search volume and low competition keywords for the word "crypto".

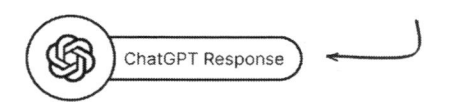

Here are five blog post ideas related to the keyword "crypto," focusing on relatively high search volume and low competition keywords:

1. "How to Buy Crypto for Beginners: A Step-by-Step Guide"
2. "Top Crypto Wallets for 2024: Safeguard Your Investments"
3. "Crypto Staking: What It Is and How to Get Started"
4. "Crypto Taxes: What You Need to Know in [Current Year]"
5. "Top Crypto Altcoins to Watch in [Current Year]"

Now that you've got your golden idea, let's give it some structure.

Example: Create a blog post outline.

Prompt: Write an outline for the blog post titled "Crypto Taxes: What You Need to Know in 2024".

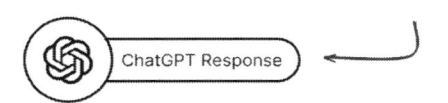

Introduction

- Hook: Briefly discuss the growing importance of cryptocurrencies in the financial world.
- Relevance: Highlight why understanding crypto taxes is essential for all crypto investors, especially with potential new regulations in 2024.
- Objective: Explain what readers can expect from the article (a comprehensive guide to navigating crypto taxes in 2024).

1. Overview of Cryptocurrency Taxation

- Definition: What constitutes a taxable event in the crypto world (e.g., trading, selling, earning interest, staking rewards).
- Taxable vs. Non-Taxable Events: Differentiate between taxable and non-taxable events in cryptocurrency transactions.

- Importance of Compliance: Emphasize the importance of reporting crypto transactions to avoid penalties.

2. Key Changes in Crypto Tax Laws for 2024

- Recent Updates: Summarize the latest updates or changes in crypto tax laws for 2024.
- Impact of Regulatory Changes: Discuss how these changes could impact crypto investors.
- New Reporting Requirements: Detail any new reporting requirements for crypto transactions (e.g., 1099 forms, international holdings).

3. How to Calculate Your Crypto Taxes

- Determining Cost Basis: Explain how to calculate the cost basis for your crypto assets.
- Methods of Calculation: FIFO (First In, First Out) vs. LIFO (Last In, First Out) vs. Specific Identification.
- Tracking Transactions: Recommend tools and software to help track and calculate crypto transactions accurately.

4. Common Tax Scenarios

- Trading Cryptocurrencies: How to report gains and losses from trading.

- Earning Crypto (Staking, Mining, Interest): Tax implications of earning crypto through various activities.
- Gifts and Donations: Tax treatment of crypto gifts and donations.
- NFTs and Taxes: Overview of how NFTs are taxed in 2024.

5. Strategies to Minimize Crypto Tax Liability

- Tax-Loss Harvesting: How to offset gains with losses.
- Long-Term vs. Short-Term Capital Gains: Explain the difference and how to benefit from long-term holding.
- Utilizing Tax-Advantaged Accounts: Discuss any opportunities to hold crypto in tax-advantaged accounts, if applicable.

6. Reporting Crypto Taxes

- Filing Requirements: Overview of the forms needed to report crypto taxes (e.g., Form 8949, Schedule D).
- Hiring a Professional: When it might make sense to consult a tax professional.
- Avoiding Common Mistakes: Highlight common errors to avoid when filing crypto taxes.

7. Consequences of Failing to Report Crypto Taxes

- Penalties and Fines: Overview of potential penalties for not reporting crypto transactions.
- IRS Crackdown: Discuss any known IRS initiatives to monitor and enforce crypto tax compliance.
- Best Practices for Compliance: Tips to ensure full compliance with tax laws.

Conclusion

- Summary of Key Points: Recap the most important information from the article.
- Final Advice: Encourage readers to stay informed and proactive about their crypto tax responsibilities.
- Call to Action: Suggest consulting a tax professional or using tax software to help manage their crypto taxes in 2024.

And just like that, you've got an outline that would make your high school English teacher weep with joy.

But why stop there? Let's take this baby home.

Example: Write a blog post section by section.

Prompt: Use the above outline to write an in-depth SEO-optimized blog post. Start with an introduction.

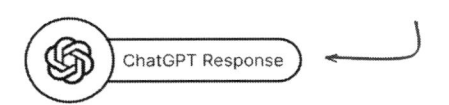

As cryptocurrencies continue to reshape the financial landscape, they bring with them not only opportunities for investment and innovation but also new challenges in areas like taxation. With 2024 expected to bring further changes to crypto tax regulations, understanding how to navigate this complex terrain has never been more important.

Whether you're trading Bitcoin, earning rewards through staking, or exploring the world of NFTs, the tax implications of your crypto activities can significantly impact your financial health. Failing to comply with tax laws can lead to hefty penalties, and the IRS is increasingly vigilant in tracking cryptocurrency transactions.

In this guide, we'll walk you through everything you need to know about crypto taxes in 2024. From recent changes in legislation to strategies for minimizing your tax liability, this comprehensive resource is designed to help you stay on the right side of the law while making the most of your crypto investments.

———————— ✺ ————————

 **Here's a pro tip to take your AI-generated content from good to holy-crap-that's-amazing:** Use ChatGPT's output as a starting point, then inject your own voice and experiences. It's like using a ghostwriter, except the ghost is a super-intelligent AI that never sleeps or asks for a raise.

So there you have it, folks - we've just scratched the surface of how ChatGPT can improve your day-to-day hustle. But hold onto your hats, because we're about to kick things into high gear.

In the next chapter, we're diving headfirst into the good stuff - how to turn ChatGPT into your own personal money-printing machine. We're talking side hustles, online businesses, and cash flows that'll make your credit card company think you've hit the jackpot.

Use ChatGPT To Earn

Passive Income

You've heard it all before, right? "Use AI to generate passive income while you sleep!" Well, let me tell you something - if making money was as easy as pushing a button, we'd all be sipping mojitos on our private islands right now.

Here's the deal: AI is changing the game, no doubt about it. It's like steroids for your business muscles. But here's where most people screw up - they think AI is some magic wand that'll turn their broke asses into millionaires overnight. WRONG.

You know those "get rich quick" schemes that promise you'll make $10k a month writing crappy listicles or generating AI art? Yeah, forget about 'em.

So what's the secret sauce? It's simple, but it ain't easy. You gotta focus on content that requires some actual brainpower - even with AI in your corner. Why? Because that's where the REAL money is, baby.

Think about it. If any schmuck with a laptop can churn out 100 blog posts a day, what do you think that content is worth? About as much as a used napkin. But if you're creating stuff that takes skill, creativity, and a dash of that special sauce called YOU... now we're talking.

Let me break it down for you. Here are the content types you should be focusing on:

1. **Ebooks:** I'm talking meaty, valuable content that people will actually pay for.
2. **SEO blogs:** Blog posts that rank and bring in that sweet, sweet organic traffic.
3. **Videos:** Use AI for ideas, and script writing, but you get to make the videos.
4. **Online courses:** Package up your knowledge into a course that solves real problems for real people.

Now, you might be thinking, "But Bernard, that sounds like a lot of work!" And you're damn right it is. **But let me ask you this:** Would you rather bust your ass for a year building something valuable, or spend the next decade chasing penny-ante schemes that barely keep the lights on?

Remember, we're playing the long game here. So, are you ready to stop playing small ball and start swinging for the fences? If so, let's freaking go!

<u>Idea 1: Sell Ebooks</u>

You're about to discover a goldmine that's been hiding right under your nose. Ebooks. Yeah, you heard me right. Those digital bundles of wisdom are your express ticket to the passive income party. And let me tell you, it's one hell of a shindig.

Now, I know what you're thinking. "But isn't the ebook market saturated?" Ha! That's like saying there are too many home runs in baseball. There's always room for another heavy hitter, my friend.

So, how do we turn this ebook dream into cold, hard cash? Let me break it down for you...

1. Pick a topic that makes people sit up and take notice.
2. Research like your financial future depends on it (because it does).
3. Organize your content so it flows like honey.
4. Create content that grabs readers by the eyeballs and doesn't let go.
5. Write in a style that resonates with your target audience.
6. Make sure your book looks slick.
7. Proofread and edit until it shines.
8. Design a cover that screams "BUY ME!"
9. Price it right.
10. Market your book like it's the next big thing (because it is).

I know what you're thinking. "That's a lot of work, Bernard!" And you're right. But don't worry, ChatGPT will help you in every step of the process.

Step 1: Find your niche and topic.

Prompt: Analyze current trends and come up with a list of emerging topics to write an ebook on.

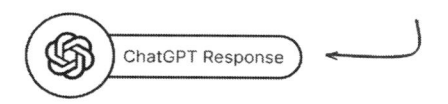

- Sustainable Living and Green Technologies
- Mental Health and Wellness
- AI and Machine Learning
- Remote Work and Digital Nomadism
- Romantic Fantasy (Romantasy)
- Personal Finance and Investing
- Natural Remedies and Alternative Medicine

Follow-up prompt: Give me concrete topics I could write about in the remote work niche.

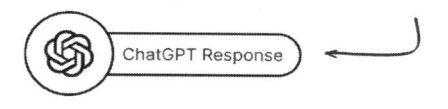

- Setting Up an Ergonomic Home Office
- Productivity Hacks for Remote Workers
- Balancing Work and Life as a Remote Worker
- Effective Communication in Remote Teams

- Mental Health and Remote Work
- Digital Nomad Lifestyle: How to Work and Travel the World
- Managing Remote Teams: Best Practices for Leaders
- Remote Work Legal Considerations
- Optimizing Virtual Meetings
- Remote Work and Career Advancement

Remember: you're not just picking a topic. You're choosing your future cash cow. So take your time, do your research, and trust your gut.

Step 2: Create an outline.

Alright, you've got your million-dollar idea. Now it's time to give it some structure.

Prompt: Create an engaging and easy-to-follow book outline for "Mental Health and Remote Work".

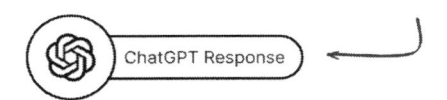

Introduction

- Overview of Remote Work Trends
- The Importance of Mental Health in the Remote Work Era
- Purpose and Scope of the Book

Chapter 1: Understanding the Mental Health Challenges of Remote Work

- The Impact of Isolation and Loneliness
- Blurred Boundaries Between Work and Personal Life
- The Pressure of Constant Connectivity
- Common Mental Health Issues Among Remote Workers (e.g., Anxiety, Depression, Burnout)

Chapter 2: Establishing a Healthy Remote Work Environment

- Creating a Routine that Supports Mental Well-being

- The Role of Physical Environment in Mental Health
- Tools and Technologies to Reduce Stress
- Importance of Breaks and Physical Activity

Step 3: Write chapter talking points.

Now we're getting into the nitty-gritty. Think of each chapter like a player on your all-star team. They need to pull their weight and contribute to the big win.

Prompt: Create talking points for "Chapter 1: Understanding the Mental Health Challenges of Remote Work"

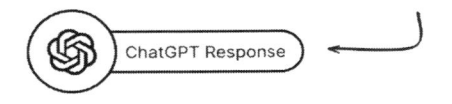

- The Impact of Isolation and Loneliness
- Blurred Boundaries Between Work and Personal Life
- The Pressure of Constant Connectivity
- Common Mental Health Issues Among Remote Workers
- Case Studies and Real-Life Examples

- Psychological Impact of Long-Term Remote Work

Step 4: Write chapter content.

Now it's time to turn those outlines into cold, hard content that'll make your readers' jaws drop.

Prompt: Using the outline above, write the full-length chapter "Understanding the Mental Health Challenges of Remote Work".

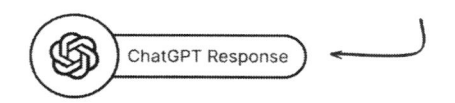

The Impact of Isolation and Loneliness

Remote work, while offering flexibility and eliminating commutes, can also lead to significant feelings of isolation. When employees work remotely, they miss out on the everyday social interactions that naturally occur in an office environment.

Casual conversations, shared coffee breaks, and the general camaraderie of being in the same space as colleagues are lost.

This lack of social interaction can lead to feelings of loneliness, which is more than just a fleeting emotion; it can have serious implications for mental health. Studies have shown that social isolation is associated with increased risks of anxiety, depression, and even physical health problems such as heart disease.

For remote workers, the absence of in-person interactions can exacerbate these issues, especially if they live alone or have limited social networks outside of work.

Blurred Boundaries Between Work and Personal Life

One of the significant challenges of remote work is the blurring of boundaries between professional and personal life. When your home is also your office, it can be difficult to separate the two. The physical boundary that typically exists between the workplace and home is gone, making it easy for work to spill over into personal time.

Remote workers often find themselves working longer hours, answering emails late into the night, or feeling guilty for not being constantly available. This erosion of boundaries can lead to burnout, a state of emotional, physical, and mental exhaustion caused by excessive and prolonged stress.

Burnout is particularly prevalent among remote workers who struggle to maintain a healthy work-life balance.

Step 5: Brainstorm the title and subtitle.

Your title is like your pick-up line. It needs to be so irresistible that readers can't help but swipe right.

Prompt: Suggest 10 variations of a catchy and memorable title and subtitle for this book.

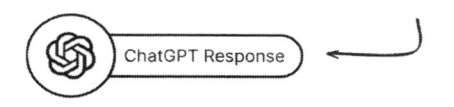

- Remote Work, Healthy Mind: Maintaining Mental Wellness in a Digital World
- The Remote Work Mindset: How to Thrive Mentally in the Home Office Era
- Mental Wellness from Afar: Navigating the Psychological Challenges of Remote Work
- Work from Home, Not Alone: Strategies for Staying Mentally Healthy in Remote Work
- Remote Work, Resilient Mind: Overcoming Mental Health Hurdles in the New Normal

- The Home Office Mentality: Balancing Productivity and Peace of Mind
- Remote Work Blues: Understanding and Conquering Mental Health Challenges
- Mindful Remote Work: Your Guide to Mental Health and Wellness from Home
- Digital Distance, Mental Strength: How to Protect Your Mental Health While Working Remotely
- Remote Work, Clear Mind: Practical Approaches to Maintaining Mental Health at Home

Remember, a great title can make or break your ebook's success. So take your time and make it count!

Step 6: Write a book description.

Alright, future bestseller, we're in the home stretch. Your Amazon book description is your sales pitch, your moment to shine, your... well, you get the idea. It's important, okay?

Prompt: Write an engaging Amazon description that will motivate potential readers to make a purchase.

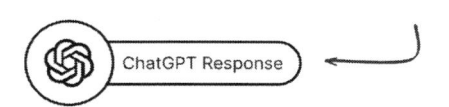

In an era where remote work has become the new normal, millions are discovering the unique challenges it brings—not just to their productivity but to their mental health. Remote Work, Healthy Mind is your essential guide to navigating these challenges with resilience and grace.

Are you feeling isolated from your colleagues? Struggling to maintain a work-life balance? Overwhelmed by the pressure to always be "on"? This book addresses these common issues head-on, offering practical strategies to help you stay mentally strong and emotionally balanced, even when your home becomes your office.

Packed with real-life examples, actionable advice, and insights from psychological research, Remote Work, Healthy Mind empowers you to create a healthy, productive work environment—no matter where you're logging in from. Whether you're a seasoned remote worker or new to the game, this book provides the tools you need to protect your mental health while thriving professionally.

Don't let the mental challenges of remote work hold you back. With Remote Work, Healthy Mind, you can transform your home office into a space where both your mind and career can flourish.

And there you have it, folks. You're now armed and dangerous, ready to conquer the ebook world.

$1M Selling AI-Generated Books.

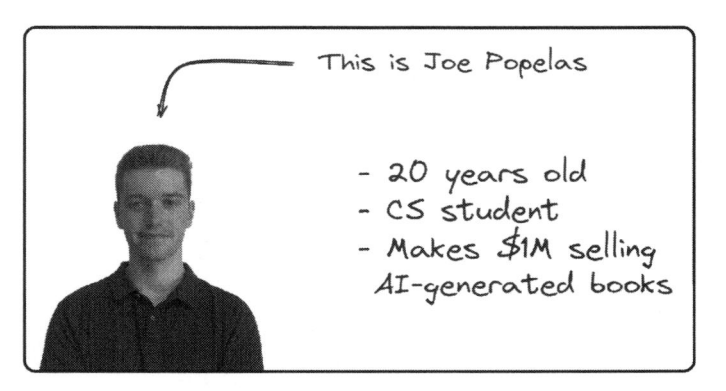

Picture this: A 20-year-old computer science student, hunched over his laptop in a cramped dorm room, churning out books faster than Stephen King on a caffeine bender.

But here's the twist – Joe isn't writing these books. He's curating and marketing them. And his audience?

Middle-aged moms scrolling through Pinterest, looking for their next beach read or self-help fix.

Now, you might be thinking, "What the hell does a college kid know about writing books for moms?" But that's the beauty of Joe's game. He doesn't need to know jack about mommy wine culture or the latest keto diet trends. All he needs is a keen eye for trends and a secret weapon: ChatGPT.

Let me explain how he does this:

First up, Joe's got a nose for profitable niches. He's not just throwing spaghetti at the wall and seeing what sticks. No, he's got a system. He dives deep into Pinterest, analyzing what's hot and what's not. Is it cozy mysteries featuring a knitting circle? Or maybe it's vegan cookbooks with a side of midlife crisis wisdom? Whatever it is, Joe's on it like white on rice.

Now, here's the twist. Joe's not writing books himself. He's using ChatGPT to do the most of the work.

Here's Joe's secret sauce:

1. Use ChatGPT to create a killer outline
2. Take each chapter and slice it up into subtopics.
3. Feed those subtopics back into ChatGPT.
4. Write individual chapters of the book one by one.

Joe's not taking shortcuts with half-baked AI output. In the early days, he personally proofread every single book. Why? Because Joe knows that quality is king. As his empire grew, Joe leveled up and hired a professional proofreader. Now he's got someone dotting those I's and crossing those T's, making sure every book is polished to perfection.

But here's the million-dollar question: How does Joe stay ahead of the game in a market so crowded? Simple. He studies his competition. That's right – Joe regularly buys books from other writers in his target niches. It's like being a secret shopper, but instead of rating customer service, he's dissecting plots and analyzing writing styles.

"What's the secret ingredient in Joe's entrepreneurial gumbo?

So what's the formula for Joe's success? It's a combination of tech, marketing, and quality. Now toss in some business savviness and holy shit – you've got a highly profitable book business.

Idea 2: Write Blog Posts

We've covered the basics of creating killer blog posts in the previous chapter. Now, let's talk about how to turn those posts into a lean, mean, money-making machine.

Here's the thing: a well-crafted blog post isn't just a one-hit-wonder. It's more like a home run that keeps circling the bases, bringing in runs (aka cash) long after you've written it. We're talking passive income, baby!

Step 1: Generate blog post ideas.

Prompt: Generate 5 ideas for a blog post about Bluetooth speakers. It's imperative that the blog post should be focusing on affiliate marketing.

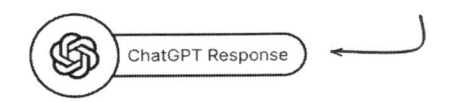

- Top 10 Bluetooth Speakers of 2024: The Ultimate Guide for Every Budget
- How to Choose the Perfect Bluetooth Speaker: Key Features to Consider Before Buying
- The Best Bluetooth Speakers for Outdoor Adventures: Durable and Portable Picks for 2024
- Bluetooth Speaker Showdown: Comparing the Best Brands in 2024
- 5 Budget-Friendly Bluetooth Speakers Under $50: Affordable Picks That Don't Compromise on Quality

---

And just like that, you've got a whole week's worth of blog post ideas.

Step 2: Generate a blog post outline.

Prompt: Generate an outline for a blog post "5 Budget-Friendly Bluetooth Speakers Under $50".

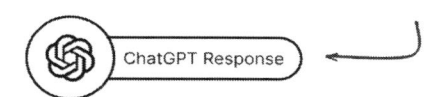

Introduction

- **Hook**: Capture the reader's attention by discussing the importance of finding a quality Bluetooth speaker without breaking the bank.
- **Purpose**: Explain that the post will highlight five top-performing Bluetooth speakers that are both affordable and of great quality.
- **Brief Overview**: Mention that these speakers have been selected based on sound quality, durability, battery life, and overall value for money.

Section 1: What to Look for in a Budget-Friendly Bluetooth Speaker

- **Sound Quality**: Discuss why sound quality matters and what to expect in the under $50 range.
- **Battery Life**: Highlight the importance of battery life for portability.

- **Durability and Build**: Mention the significance of build quality, including features like waterproofing.
- **Portability**: Discuss size and weight considerations for a Bluetooth speaker intended for travel or outdoor use.
- **Extra Features**: Mention additional features that might be available, like hands-free calling, Bluetooth range, or voice assistant compatibility.

Remember, you're the manager here. If you don't like what you see, call for a change-up. Tweak, adjust, and refine until you've got an outline that makes you want to stand up and cheer.

Step 3: Write a blog post.

Prompt: Write an engaging, SEO-optimized blog post titled "5 Budget-Friendly Bluetooth Speakers Under $50" using the outline above.

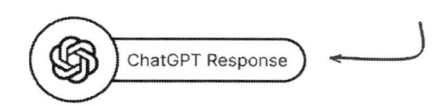

5 Budget-Friendly Bluetooth Speakers Under $50

When it comes to finding the perfect Bluetooth speaker, you don't have to spend a fortune to get great sound quality and reliable performance. Whether you're looking for a portable speaker to take on your next adventure or just a budget-friendly option for everyday use, there are plenty of options under $50 that deliver exceptional value.

In this post, we'll explore five of the best budget-friendly Bluetooth speakers available in 2024, offering top-notch features without breaking the bank.

What to Look for in a Budget-Friendly Bluetooth Speaker

Before diving into our top picks, it's important to understand what to look for in a budget-friendly Bluetooth speaker. Even at a lower price point, there are key features that can make or break your listening experience.

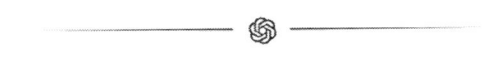

When ChatGPT serves up that shiny new blog post, don't just copy-paste and call it a day. Instead, think of it as your first draft. It's got the bones, but now it's your job to add the meat.

Inject your personality. Throw in some personal stories about listening to music with your friends on a camping trip. Sprinkle in those affiliate links like you're salting a perfectly grilled campfire steak. And for the love of all that's holy, don't forget to optimize for SEO.

Remember, ChatGPT is your assistant, not your ghostwriter. Use it to get the ball rolling, but make sure the final product screams YOU.

Building a profitable blog with AI.

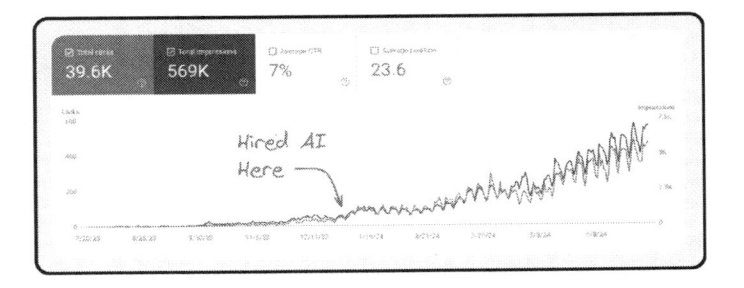

This story is about yours truly, AKA me.

On October 15, 2023, I launched my new website with shaky hands and a racing heart. I'd done my homework, sure. Spent weeks researching, planning, and setting up a website that didn't look like it was designed by a colorblind toddler.

But let's be real - the hardest part was staring me in the face like an angry bouncer at an exclusive club: how the hell do I get people through the digital door?

Now, I'm no SEO rookie. I've been in the trenches, optimizing pages, coming up with catchy titles, and writing meta descriptions. But this time, I wanted to do something different. Something that would make the SEO gods sit up and take notice.

I had two choices: I could grind out blog posts until my fingers fell off, or I could hire a team of writers and watch my bank account shrivel. Neither option had me jumping for joy.

That's when it hit me like a double shot of espresso at 3 AM: Why not let AI do the heavy lifting?

For six months, ChatGPT and I have been writing blog posts together. And let me tell you, the results are enough to make SEO veterans weep tears of joy.

We're talking 50,000 visitors, folks. 15,000 monthly clicks. And the growth? It's steady and growing every month. So, what's this website about?

Image this: You need a ChatGPT prompt to write a product description. Or do you want to write a blog post that ranks on Google? I've got you covered. The website is called Prompt Advance and it has ChatGPT prompts for anything you can image.

Right now, the site is as free as advice from your uncle. Why? Because I'm focusing on growth. And the target? 100,000 monthly visitors. That's the magic number I want to achieve.

Once we hit that, then we're talking monetization. Once we crack that 100K ceiling, the sky's the limit. We're talking premium prompts, AI-powered courses, maybe even a "Build Your Own AI Content Empire" masterclass. The possibilities are enough to keep me up at night - in a good way this time.

Here's the bottom line, folks: these exciting days, you've got two choices. You can cling to the old ways, pumping out content like it's 2010 and hoping for the best. Or you can saddle up, embrace the AI revolution, and blaze a trail into the future.

Idea 3: Make Videos

While everyone else is slaving away at their 9-to-5 jobs, smart entrepreneurs are earning cash while they sleep, all thanks to the power of YouTube.

Now, I know what you're thinking. "But Bernard, isn't blogging the way to go for passive income?" Ha! That's like saying flip phones are the future of communication. Sure, blogging has its place, but YouTube? It's the heavy hitter, the Babe Ruth of content creation.

Why? Because people are lazy, my friend. They'd rather watch a video than read an article any day of the week.

So, how do you get started on this YouTube journey? Let's break it down, step by step.

Step 1: Generate video ideas.

Think about what people are searching for, what problems they need solved. Are they looking for ways to make money online? (Hint: they always are.) Are they trying to learn a new skill?

Find the intersection of what you know and what people want to know. That's your sweet spot.

Prompt: Act as a YouTube research analyst. Generate 5 ideas for a high search, low competition video idea.

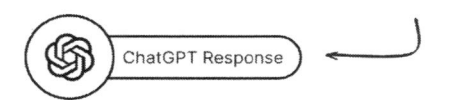

1. How to Organize a Small Apartment on a Budget
2. Beginner's Guide to Understanding Cryptocurrency Wallets
3. DIY No-Sew Clothing Hacks for Fashion Emergencies
4. Simple Vegan Meal Prep for a Week Under $50
5. How to Create a Professional-Looking Resume with Free Tools

Step 2: Generate a video script.

Next, you've gotta write that video script.

Prompt: Generate an engaging 500-word long YouTube video script for "Beginner's Guide to Understanding Cryptocurrency Wallets".

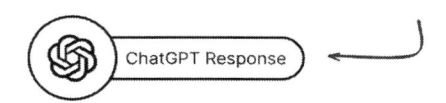
ChatGPT Response

[INTRO]

[Upbeat background music plays]

[Host on camera] "Hey everyone! Welcome back to [Your Channel Name], your go-to spot for all things crypto and tech! If you're new here, don't forget to hit that subscribe button and ring the bell to stay updated on our latest videos. Today, we're diving into a super important topic for anyone new to the world of cryptocurrency—understanding cryptocurrency wallets. Whether you're just getting started with Bitcoin or exploring other digital currencies, this guide is for you!"

[CUT TO GRAPHIC: 'What is a Cryptocurrency Wallet?']

[Host Voiceover] "So, what exactly is a cryptocurrency wallet? Think of it like a digital bank account for your cryptocurrencies. It's a tool that allows you to store, send, and receive digital currencies like Bitcoin, Ethereum, and many others. But unlike a traditional bank account, a crypto wallet doesn't store money in the traditional sense. Instead, it stores something called 'private keys,' which are basically secret codes that allow you to access your cryptocurrency on the blockchain."

Now, I can already hear some of you whining. "But Bernard, I don't want to be on camera!" or "I'm not good at editing!" But guess what? AI is here to save your sorry behind.

Enter InVideoAI a video creation platform that does all the heavy lifting for you. You pick a template, throw in your script, and BAM! The AI works its magic, generating visuals, adding voiceovers, and even suggesting content. It's so easy, even your technologically challenged grandma could use it.

Before you go off and create an AI-generated video empire, there's something you need to know. YouTube isn't too keen on fully AI-generated content. They're like that annoying teacher who always checks for plagiarism. If they catch you using 100% AI-generated videos, you can kiss your monetization goodbye.

So here's the million-dollar tip (literally): Use the AI as a starting point, but add your own secret sauce. Record your own voiceover, throw in some personal anecdotes, maybe even show yourself on camera for a few seconds. Make it uniquely yours. That way, you're not just following the rules — you're playing the game like a pro.

Idea 4: Create Online Courses

Ever wondered how some schmucks manage to make six figures while lounging on a beach, sipping Margaritas? Well, it can be easily done by selling online courses.

Now, I know what you're thinking. "I'm not an expert in anything, I can't teach!" First off, cut that crap out. Everyone's an expert in something. And second, who says you need to be an expert when you've got AI in your corner?

ChatGPT has more knowledge than a library full of nerds. And guess what? It's your best friend in the online course game.

So, how do we leverage this bad boy to create a course that'll have people throwing money at their screens? Let's break it down.

Step 1: Generate online course ideas.

Feed ChatGPT info about your skills and interests, and watch it spit out course ideas that actually have market potential.

Prompt: Generate 5 ideas for creating a profitable online course based on my [skills] and [interests]. My skills and interests are: writing, and building websites.

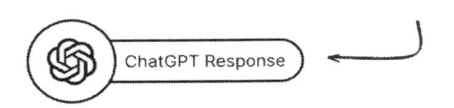

1. "Portfolio Perfection: Showcase Your Skills with a Personal Website"
2. "Website Copywriting Mastery: Write Words that Sell"
3. "The Freelancer's Guide: Writing and Building Websites for Clients"
4. "Monetize Your Passion: Building and Writing for Niche Websites"
5. "From Blank Page to Blog: Writing and Building Your First Website"

Step 2: Create a course curriculum.

Now, onto the course structure.

Prompt: Create a logical and engaging course structure for "From Blank Page to Blog: Writing and Building Your First Website" that will keep learners engaged. Include sections, lectures, and quizzes.

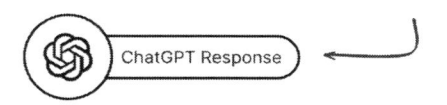

ChatGPT Response

Section 1: Introduction to Blogging

Lecture 1.1: Why Start a Blog?

- Overview of the benefits of blogging
- Different types of blogs (personal, professional, niche)
- Setting goals for your blog

Lecture 1.2: Finding Your Niche and Target Audience

- How to choose a blog niche
- Identifying and understanding your target audience
- Conducting competitor analysis

Quiz 1: Identifying Your Blog's Purpose and Audience

Section 2: Building Your Blog

Lecture 2.1: Choosing a Blogging Platform

- Overview of popular platforms (WordPress, Blogger, etc.)
- Choosing the right platform for your needs
- Setting up your domain and hosting

Lecture 2.2: Setting Up Your Blog

- Installing WordPress (or chosen platform)
- Selecting and customizing a theme
- Configuring essential plugins and settings

Lecture 2.3: Navigating the Backend: Dashboard, Posts, and Pages

- Introduction to the blog's backend interface
- Creating and managing posts and pages
- Understanding categories, tags, and menus

Quiz 2: Platform Selection and Blog Setup Basics

Step 3: Create videos.

Remember that video script stuff we talked about in the previous chapter? Well, guess what? We're about to use it.

It can help you craft scripts that'll make your viewers think you're the love child of Tony Robbins and Warren Buffett. And the best part? You can use that InVideoAI we talked about to turn those scripts into slick videos.

But wait, there's more! (God, I sound like an infomercial.) ChatGPT can help you create quizzes and assessments that'll make your students feel like they're actually learning something. Because let's face it, if they feel smart, they'll keep coming back for more.

Step 4: Create quizzes.

Prompt: Create a quiz with 10 questions about "Lecture 2.2: Setting Up Your Blog" Use a combination of multiple choice questions, and yes/no questions.

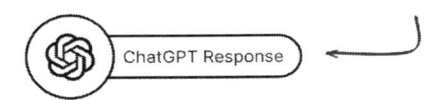 ChatGPT Response

1. What is the first step in setting up your blog after choosing a platform?

- A) Writing your first blog post
- B) Customizing your theme
- C) Installing the platform (e.g., WordPress)
- D) Setting up an email list

Answer: C) Installing the platform (e.g., WordPress)

2. Which of the following is NOT a factor to consider when selecting a theme for your blog?

- A) Responsiveness (mobile-friendly design)
- B) Color of the theme
- C) Customization options
- D) Integration with social media

Answer: B) Color of the theme

3. True or False: It's important to configure essential plugins after setting up your blog.

- A) True
- B) False

Answer: A) True

Step 4: Marketing.

Now, let's talk marketing. Because a course without students is like a Ferrari without gas – looks pretty, but ain't going nowhere. ChatGPT can help you craft email sequences, social media posts, and ad copy that'll have people tripping over themselves to sign up. It's like having Don Draper on speed dial, minus the drinking problem.

Hint: you already learned to do all of these in previous chapters.

Step 4: Publishing.

So, you've got your course. You've got your marketing. Now where do you put this golden goose? Platforms like Udemy, Skillshare, Teachable, Thinkific, or Kajabi are your new best friends.

They handle all the tech stuff, so you can focus on counting your money.

Now, I'm not gonna sit here and tell you you'll make a million bucks overnight. That's what those scammy gurus do, and we're better than that. But I will say this: with a solid course, smart marketing, and the power of AI, you've got a real shot at building a passive income stream that could change your life.

$175,000 teaching people how to use AI.

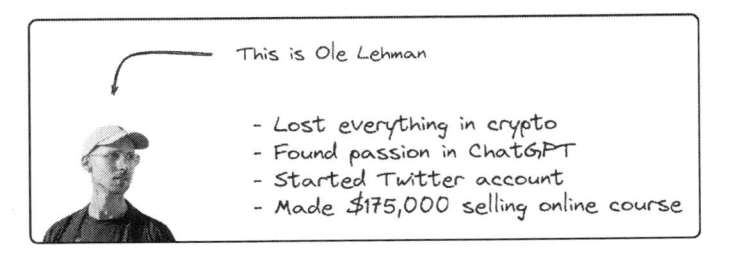

This is Ole Lehman

- Lost everything in crypto
- Found passion in ChatGPT
- Started Twitter account
- Made $175,000 selling online course

On November 11, 2022, Ole Lehman watched in horror as his entire crypto portfolio evaporated. The market crash wiped out everything he'd built over the past years. Just like that, he went from crypto mogul to broke-as-hell nobody.

But here's the thing: sometimes, when you lose everything, you stumble onto something even bigger.

Ole had been all-in on crypto. He'd rode the waves, survived the dips, and thought he had it all figured out. He was the guy everyone came to for trading advice, the one who could spot a pump-and-dump from a mile away. Until he couldn't.

The crash hit him like a freight train. One minute, he was planning his early retirement. The next, he was wondering how he'd pay rent. Ole spent weeks in a daze, questioning every decision he'd ever made. He felt like a fraud, a failure, a cautionary tale.

Then, on November 30, 2022, OpenAI dropped a bomb called ChatGPT. And just like that, the game changed.

Why did this catch Ole's eye? Simple. The hype, the potential, the wild possibilities... it all felt eerily familiar. It was crypto all over again, but this time, with brains instead of coins.

Ole didn't waste time. By December 5, he was knee-deep in AI Twitter, posting hot takes and predictions. He'd wake up at 5 AM, chug coffee, and spend hours exploring ChatGPT. It was like trading all over again - spotting trends, analyzing patterns, always looking for the next big thing.

On January 1, 2023, Ole made a decision. He wasn't going to be just another voice in the AI echo chamber. He was going to build something real. That's when he started posting about his journey on Twitter. He called it "The AI Solopreneur".

As his audience grew, Ole noticed something. These weren't just followers; they were hungry entrepreneurs looking for guidance. And just like that, a business idea clicked into place.

For six weeks straight, Ole worked 16-hour days. He poured everything he knew about AI, audience building, and digital marketing into a comprehensive course. He called it "The AI Audience Accelerator" - a step-by-step blueprint for building a rabid following using AI tools.

On March 15, 2023, Ole launched the course. His palms were sweaty, his heart was racing. What if no one bought it? What if they all called him out as a fraud?

The results blew his mind. In the first month, he had 1,078 orders. $176,885 in gross revenue. It was more money than he'd ever made in a single day of crypto trading.

Why did it work? Ole believes it's because he wasn't just selling a course. He was selling a lifeline to entrepreneurs drowning in the noise of the digital age. He was offering a way to stand out, to build something meaningful in a world of AI-generated bullshit.

And here's my favorite part. He's not pretending to be some AI genius or marketing wizard. He's just a guy who lost everything, spotted an opportunity, and worked his ass off to make it happen. His real expertise? Spotting trends and moving fast. That's the secret sauce, folks. The ability to pivot, to reinvent yourself, to turn disaster into opportunity.

Use ChatGPT To Make Money Online

If you've been hustling on platforms like Fiverr, or Upwork, you know the freelance game can be brutal. It's a dog-eat-dog world out there, and standing out from the pack is tougher than ever. But here's where ChatGPT comes in.

Let me break it down for you, starting with the bread and butter of many freelancers.

Idea 1: Copywriting

Picture this: You land a gig writing email copy for a client's marketing campaign. In the past, you'd be staring at a blank screen, scratching your head for that perfect hook. But now? You've got ChatGPT in your corner.

Here's a real-world example. Let's say you're writing an email to promote a new fitness program. You could hit up ChatGPT with something like this:

"Write an email using the AIDA framework to promote a 12-week body transformation program called 'Shred It!' targeting busy professionals who want to get in shape fast."

BAM! In seconds, you've got a solid foundation to work with. Now, here's where your skills come in. You take that raw material, inject your personality, tweak it to match the client's voice, and voila! You've just cut your writing time in half.

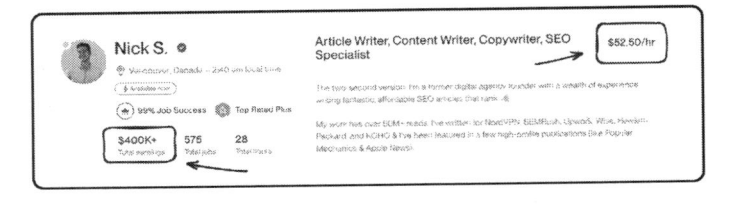

A decent copywriter might charge $100-$200 for a single marketing email. With ChatGPT, you could potentially churn out twice as many in the same time. Do the math, folks. We're talking about DOUBLING your income potential. If that's not a walk-off win, I don't know what is.

Idea 2: Writing Blog Posts

Moving on to blog posts. We've all been there - staring at the screen, willing words to appear. It's like trying to squeeze water from a rock. But with ChatGPT? It's like turning on a fire hose of ideas.

Remember how we used ChatGPT for brainstorming topics, creating outlines, and even generating content? Apply that same process to blog writing, and watch your productivity soar. You can knock out a 1000-word post in a fraction of the time it used to take.

A typical freelance blogger might charge $0.10 to $0.20 per word. That's $100 to $200 for a 1000-word post. Now, imagine you could write three posts in the time it used to take to write one. Suddenly, your earning potential jumps from $600 a day to $1800. That's not chump change, my friend. That's the difference between scraping by and living large.

But here's the kicker: it's not just about the money. It's about time. Time you can spend landing more clients, improving your skills, or hell, maybe even taking a vacation. When was the last time you heard a freelancer talk about having free time?

Idea 3: Ghostwriting

Now, let's talk about the stealth bomber of the writing world: ghostwriting. This is where the big bucks are, folks. And with ChatGPT, you're about to become a ghostwriting ninja.

Let's say you land a gig writing a non-fiction e-book on personal finance. In the past, you'd be buried in research for weeks. But now? You've got ChatGPT to help you outline chapters, generate ideas, and even flesh out key concepts.

Here's a pro tip: Use ChatGPT to create a detailed outline, then have it expand on each point. You'll end up with a rough draft faster than you can say "bestseller." Of course, you'll need to edit, refine, and inject your client's voice - but you've just cut your writing time by 50% or more.

A 30,000-word e-book might net you anywhere from $3000 to $10,000, depending on your experience and the client. With ChatGPT, you could potentially take on two or three of these projects instead of just one. Do I need to spell out what that means for your bank account?

Idea 4: Interpreting

If you're bilingual (or multilingual), ChatGPT is about to become your new best friend. Translation services are in high demand, and ChatGPT can give you a serious edge.

Let's say you're translating a website from English to Spanish. You could use ChatGPT to generate a first draft of the translation, then apply your language expertise to refine and perfect it. It's like having a super-smart bilingual intern who works for free and doesn't complain.

But here's the catch - and pay attention, because this is important. You NEED to be fluent in both languages to make this work. ChatGPT is good, but it's not perfect. If you try to fake it, you'll get caught faster than a kid with his hand in the cookie jar. Use ChatGPT as a tool, not a crutch.

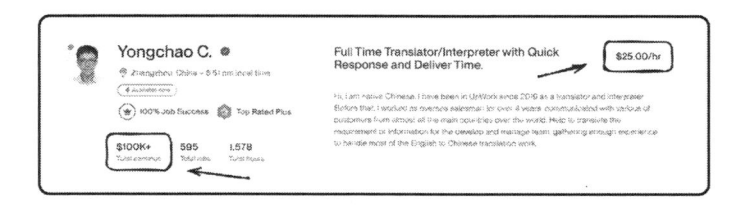

Translation services can earn serious cash. We're talking $0.10 to $0.20 per word, sometimes more for specialized content. With ChatGPT speeding up your process, you could potentially double your output.

The Sky's the Limit

Look, I've barely scratched the surface here. ChatGPT can help with all sorts of freelance gigs - from social media posts to product descriptions, from scriptwriting to SEO optimization. The possibilities are as endless as your imagination.

Here's the bottom line: ChatGPT isn't just a tool. It's a freakin' revolution for freelancers. It's like strapping a jet pack to your business. You'll work faster, produce more, and have the potential to earn WAY more than you ever thought possible.

But remember this: ChatGPT is powerful, but it's not magic. You still need your skills, your creativity, and your human touch. It's not about replacing you - it's about supercharging you.

Last Words

Holy smokes, we've covered more ground than a marathon runner on steroids. From cranking out killer content to building passive income empires, we've unlocked the secret weapon that's about to turn the business world on its head.

Whether you're a wet-behind-the-ears newbie or a grizzled business veteran, a lone-wolf freelancer or a cubicle-dwelling dreamer, ChatGPT is about to become your new best friend. Hell, it's more than a friend - it's your personal army of content-creating, money-making, time-saving ninjas all rolled into one.

Think about it - how much is your time worth? Because ChatGPT is about to give you a big fat refund on hours wasted staring at a blank screen. And money? Forget about it. The cost savings here are bigger than Texas. You're getting the output of a whole marketing department for less than the price of a decent cup of coffee.

Now, I've handed you the keys to the kingdom. I've shown you the prompts, the techniques, the hacks that'll put you lightyears ahead of the competition. But here's the kicker - you gotta use 'em. This isn't some get-rich-quick scheme where you can sit on your ass and watch the money roll in. You need to put in the work, apply these strategies, and make ChatGPT dance to your tune.

Let me leave you with this: ChatGPT isn't just a tool, it's a revolution. It's like having Edison's lightbulb before electricity went mainstream. You're standing at the forefront of a new era, my friend. As the great Wayne Gretzky once said, "I skate to where the puck is going to be, not where it has been." Well, ChatGPT is where the puck is going, and you're holding the damn hockey stick.

So what are you waiting for? The future is here, and it's powered by AI. It's time to stop watching from the sidelines and get in the game. With ChatGPT, you're not just playing - you're winning. Now go out there and show the world what you're made of. Game on!

Thank You!

Thanks for sticking around to the end! You've just finished a journey that could change your life for good.

I put a lot of effort into this book, and I genuinely hope it's given you some valuable insights and tools. My goal was to spark your creativity and show you the potential of ChatGPT in your work and business ventures.

I'm rooting for your success. Whether you're looking to boost your freelance career, start a new business, or just work more efficiently, I hope this book gives you a solid foundation to build on.

If you found this book helpful, I'd really appreciate it if you could leave an honest review on Amazon. Your feedback not only helps me improve but also helps other potential readers decide if this book is right for them.

Your support means a lot to me. It's readers like you who make the long hours of writing and research worthwhile.

Thanks again for your time and attention. I truly appreciate you giving this book a chance.

Wishing you all the best in your future endeavors,

Bernard!

Made in the USA
Columbia, SC
09 September 2024

42029868R00050